THE GUITAR

3 Chord Songbook

PLAY 50 GREAT SONGS WITH ONLY 3 EASY CHORDS

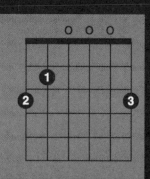

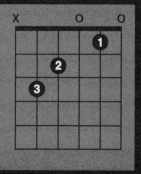

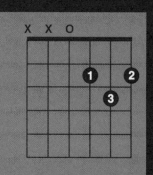

ISBN 978-1-4803-9970-9

HAL•LEONARD®
CORPORATION

7777 W. BLUEMOUND RD. P.O. BOX 13819 MILWAUKEE, WI 53213

3 Chord Songbook

PLAY 50 GREAT SONGS WITH ONLY 3 EASY CHORDS

Contents

All Right Now

Words and Music by Andy Fraser and Paul Rodgers

%️ **Verse**

Moderately

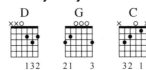

1. There she stood in the street, _ smil - in' from her head _ to her
(2., 3.) *See additional lyrics*

feet. I said - a, "Hey, now, what is this? _ Now, ba - by, may - be, may -

- be she's in need _ of a kiss." I said - a, "Hey, _____ what's your

name, _ ba - by? May - be we can see things the same. Now don't you

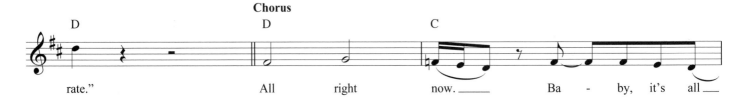

wait _____ or hes - i - tate. _____ Let's move be - fore they raise the park - ing

Chorus

rate." All right now. _ Ba - by, it's all _

To Coda ⊕

_ right _ now. _____ All right now. _ Ba - by, it's all _

Additional Lyrics

2., 3. I took her home to my place,
Watchin' ev'ry move on her face.
She said, "Look, what's your game, baby?
Are you tryin' to put me in shame?"
I said a, "Slow, don't go so fast.
Don't you think that love can last?"
She said, "Love? Lord above.
Ooh, now you're tryin' to trick me in love."

Amanda

Words and Music by Bob McDill

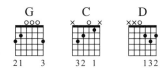

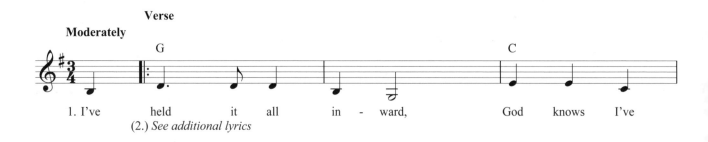

Verse

Moderately

1. I've held it all in - ward, God knows I've
(2.) *See additional lyrics*

tried,   but it's an aw - ful a - wak - 'ning   in a

coun - try boy's ___ life   to look in ___ the

mir - ror in to - tal sur - prise ___   at the hair on my shoul-

-ders,   the age in my eyes.   A -

Chorus

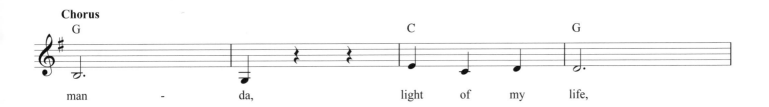

man -   da,   light of my life,

fate should have made you   a gen - tle - man's wife.

A - man -   da, _____ light of my

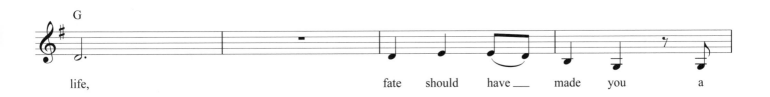

life,   fate should have made you   a

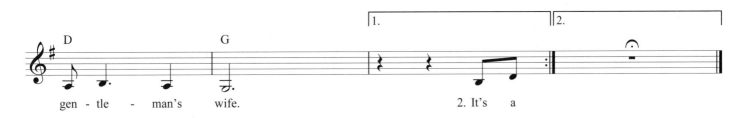

gen - tle - man's wife.   2. It's a

Additional Lyrics

2. It's a measure of people who don't understand
   The pleasures of life in a hillbilly band.
   I got my first guitar when I was fourteen.
   Well, I finally made forty, still wearing jeans.

At the Hop

Words and Music by Arthur Singer, John Madara and David White

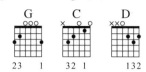

Verse

Brightly

1. Well, you can rock it, you can roll it, do the stomp and e - ven stroll it at the hop.
(2.) *See additional lyrics*

When the rec - ords start a - spin - nin', you ca - lyp - so and you chick - en at the hop.

Do the dance sen - sa - tions that are sweep - in' the na - tion at the hop.

Chorus

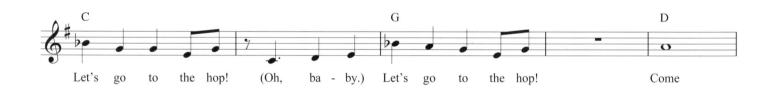

Let's go to the hop! Let's go to the hop! (Oh, ba - by.)

Let's go to the hop! (Oh, ba - by.) Let's go to the hop! Come

on, let's go to the hop! 2. Well, you can 3. Well, you can

Verse

rock it, you can roll it, do the stomp and e-ven stroll it at the hop. When the
(4.) *See additional lyrics*

rec-ords start a-spin-nin', you ca-lyp-so and you chick-en at the hop. Do the

dance sen-sa-tions that are sweep-in' the na-tion at the hop. 4. You _____ can

hop. Let's go! ___ Let's go to the hop! Let's go to the hop!

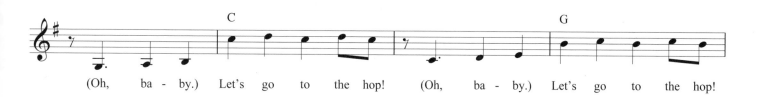

(Oh, ba-by.) Let's go to the hop! (Oh, ba-by.) Let's go to the hop!

Come on, let's go to the hop!

Additional Lyrics

2., 4. Well, you can swing it, you can groove it,
You can really start to move it at the hop.
Where the jockey is the smoothest
And the music is the coolest at the hop.
All the cats and the chicks can get their kicks at the hop.

Betty Lou's Gettin' Out Tonight

Words and Music by Bob Seger

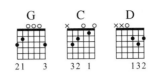

Verse

Bright Rock 'n' Roll beat

1. Have you heard the news? _ It's all o - ver town. _
2. First heard the ru - mor down on Twelfth _ and Main. _

If you ain't heard it, boys, you bet - ter sit down. I got the sto - ry here. It's
The poor _ drug - gist, he was go - in' in - sane. His stuff is sell - ing out like

hot off the press. _ Brace your - self, now, and take a deep breath.
nev - er be - fore. _ He fi - n'lly had to up and close _ the store.

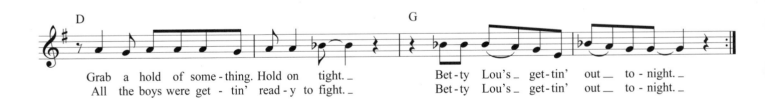

Grab a hold of some - thing. Hold on tight. _ Bet - ty Lou's _ get - tin' out _ to - night. _
All the boys were get - tin' read - y to fight. _ Bet - ty Lou's _ get - tin' out _ to - night. _

% Chorus

Bet - ty Lou's _ get - tin' out _ to - night. _ Bet - ty Lou's _ get - tin'

out _ to - night. _ She was bad. Her mom - ma got mad.

But now her mom-ma says it's all___ right. ___ All the boys are get-tin'

read-y and right. ___ Bet-ty Lou's___ get-tin' out___ to-night. ___

Bridge

(Instrumental) Bet - ty Lou.

Bet - ty Lou.
It's all true.
Yes, it's true.

To Coda ⊕

It's real - ly true.
Bet - ty Lou.

D.S. al Coda

(Spoken:) What do you think about that, boys?

⊕ **Coda**

Outro-Chorus

Well, _____

Bet - ty Lou's _ get - tin' out ___ to - night. _

Bet - ty Lou's _ get - tin' out ___ to - night. _   She was bad.   Her

mom - ma got mad.   But now her mom - ma says   it's all ___ right. ___

All   the boys are get - tin' read - y and right. ___   Bet - ty Lou's _ get - tin'

out ___ to - night. _   Her mom - ma said that it would be all   right. _

Bet - ty Lou's _ get - tin' out ___ to - night. _   Grab a hold of some - thing.

Hold on tight. _   Bet - ty Lou's _ get - tin' out ___ to - night. _

Bad Moon Rising

Words and Music by John Fogerty

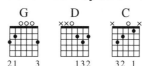

Verse

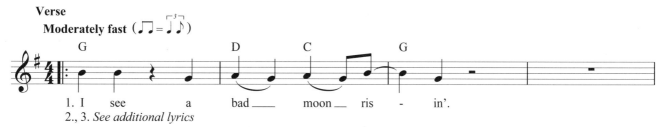

1. I see a bad _____ moon _____ ris - in'.
2., 3. *See additional lyrics*

I see trou - ble on the way. _____ I see

earth - quakes and light - nin'. I see bad _____ times to - day. _____

Chorus

_____ Don't go a - round to - night. _____ Well, it's

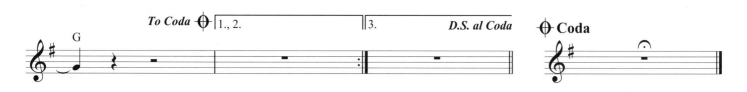

bound to take _____ your life. _____ There's a bad _____ moon on the rise. _____

To Coda ⊕   1., 2.   3.   ***D.S. al Coda***   ⊕ **Coda**

_____

Additional Lyrics

2. I hear hurricanes a-blowin'.
   I know the end is comin' soon.
   I fear rivers overflowin'.
   I hear the voice of rage and ruin.

3. Hope you got your things together.
   Hope you are quite prepared to die.
   Looks like we're in for nasty weather.
   One eye is taken for an eye.

Blowin' in the Wind

Words and Music by Bob Dylan

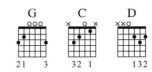

Verse
Moderately fast

1. How man-y roads ___ must a man ___ walk ___ down ___
2., 3. *See additional lyrics*

___ be - fore ___ you call ___ him a man? ___

How man-y seas ___ must a white ___ dove ___ sail ___

___ be - fore ___ she sleeps in the sand? ___

Yes, and how ___ man-y times ___ must the can -

non - balls ___ fly _____ be - fore _____ they are for -

- ev - er banned? _ The an -

Chorus

- swer, my friend, ___ is blow - in' in ___ the wind. ___

___ The an - swer is blow - in' in ___ the wind. ___

1., 2.   3.

___

Additional Lyrics

2. How many years can a mountain exist
Before it is washed to the sea?
How many years can some people exist
Before they're allowed to be free?
Yes, and how many times can a man turn his head
And pretend that he just doesn't see?

3. How many times must a man look up
Before he can see the sky?
How many ears must one man have
Before he can hear people cry?
Yes, and how many deaths will it take till he knows
That too many people have died?

Blue Moon of Kentucky

Words and Music by Bill Monroe

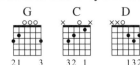

% Chorus

Moderate Waltz

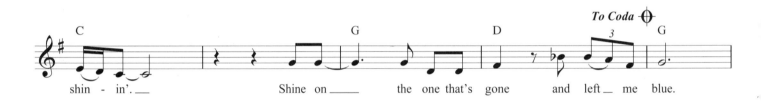

Blue moon of Ken - tuck - y, keep on shin - in'. ___ Shine on ___

___ the one that's gone and proved ___ un - true. Blue ___ moon of Ken - tuck - y, keep on

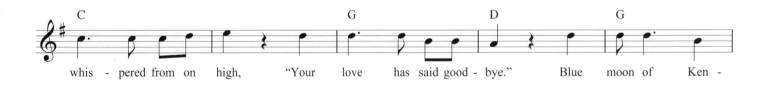

shin - in'. ___ Shine on ___ the one that's gone and left ___ me blue.

Verse

It was on a moon - light night, the stars were shin - in' bright, and they

whis - pered from on high, "Your love has said good - bye." Blue moon of Ken -

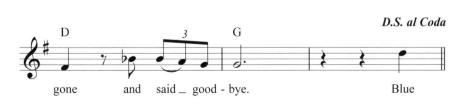

tuck - y, keep on shin - in'. ___ Shine on ___ the one that's

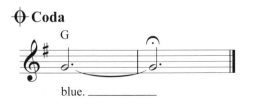

gone and said ___ good - bye. Blue   blue. _____

For What It's Worth

Words and Music by Stephen Stills

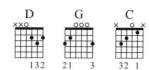

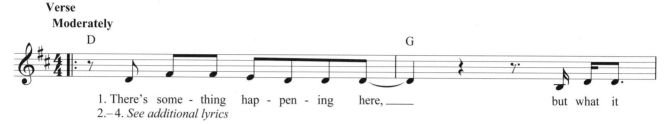

Verse
Moderately

1. There's some-thing hap-pen-ing here, _____ but what it
2.–4. *See additional lyrics*

is ain't ex-act-ly clear. _____ There's a man with a gun o-ver there _____

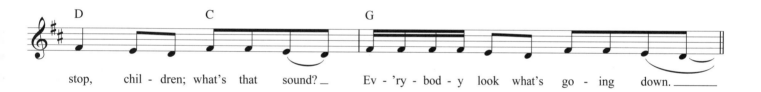

_____ tell-ing me I've got to be-ware. _____ I think it's time we

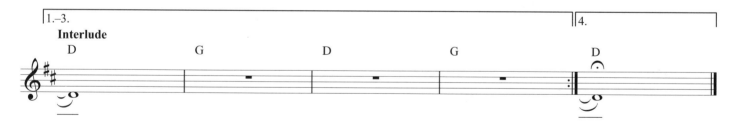

stop, chil-dren; what's that sound? _ Ev-'ry-bod-y look what's go-ing down. _____

1.–3.
Interlude

4.

Additional Lyrics

2. There's battle lines being drawn.
   Nobody's right if everybody's wrong.
   Young people speaking their minds,
   Getting so much resistance from behind.
   I think it's time we stop; hey, what's that sound?
   Ev'rybody look what's going down.

3. What a field day for the heat.
   A thousand people in the street,
   Singing songs and carrying signs,
   Mostly say, "Hooray for our side."
   It's time we stop; hey, what's that sound?
   Ev'rybody look what's going down.

4. Paranoia strikes deep.
   Into your life it will creep.
   It starts when you're always afraid.
   You step out of line, the man come and take you away.
   We better stop; hey, what's that sound?
   Ev'rybody look what's going down.

Bluejean Bop

Words and Music by Gene Vincent and Hal Levy

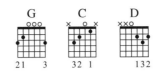

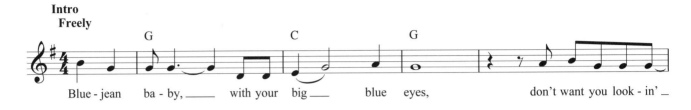

Intro
Freely

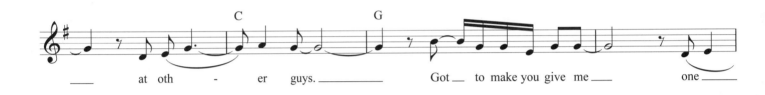

Blue - jean ba - by, ____ with your big ____ blue eyes, don't want you look - in' ____

____ at oth - er guys. ____ Got ____ to make you give me ____ one

Fast Rock

____ more chance. ____ I can't keep still, so, ba - by, let's dance. 1. Well, the

Verse

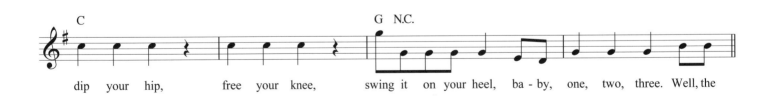

blue - jean bop is the bop for me. ____ Well, it's the bop ____ that's done in dun - ga - ree. ____ You

dip your hip, free your knee, swing it on your heel, ba - by, one, two, three. Well, the

𝄋 Chorus

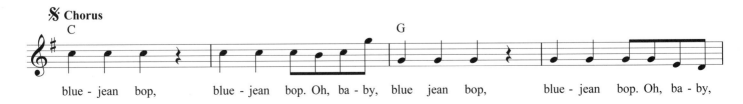

blue - jean bop, blue - jean bop. Oh, ba - by, blue jean bop, blue - jean bop. Oh, ba - by,

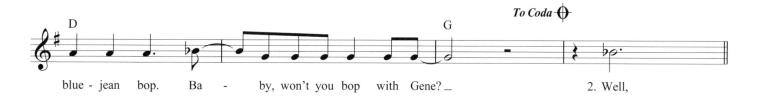

blue - jean bop. Ba - by, won't you bop with Gene? _ 2. Well,

Verse

blue - jean ba - by, when I bop with you, _ well, my heart starts a - hop - pin' like a,

a kan - ga - roo. My feet do things they nev - er done be - fore. _ Well- a, blue - jean ba - by, give me

D.S. al Coda   **Coda**   **Outro**

more, more, more. Well, the   Well, it's a blue - jean, a

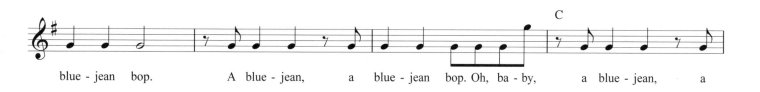

blue - jean bop. A blue - jean, a blue - jean bop. Oh, ba - by, a blue - jean, a

blue - jean bop, a blue - jean, a blue - jean bop. A blue - jean, oh,

ba - by, won't you bop with Gene? _

A Boy Named Sue

Words and Music by Shel Silverstein

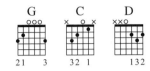

Moderately bright

Verse

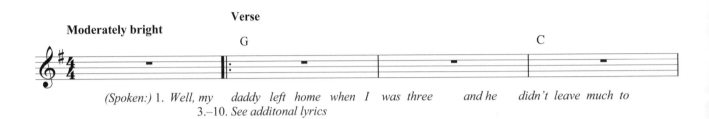

(Spoken:) 1. Well, my daddy left home when I was three and he didn't leave much to
3.–10. *See additonal lyrics*

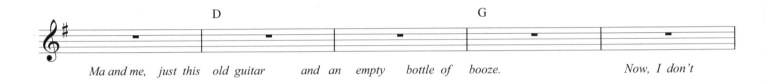

Ma and me, just this old guitar and an empty bottle of booze. Now, I don't

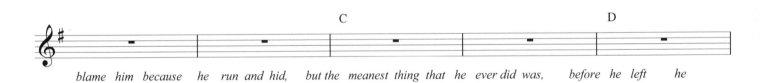

blame him because he run and hid, but the meanest thing that he ever did was, before he left he

Verse

went and named me Sue. 2. Well, he must have thought it was

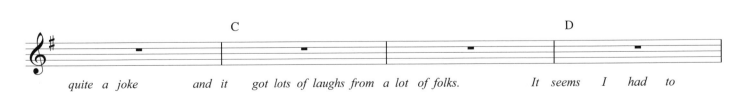

quite a joke and it got lots of laughs from a lot of folks. It seems I had to

fight my whole life through.   *Some gal would giggle and I'd get red, and some*

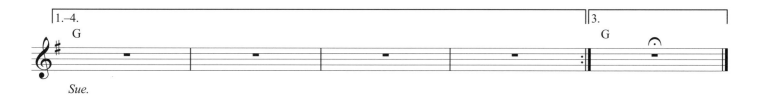

guy would laugh and I'd bust his head.   *I tell you, life ain't easy for a boy named*

Sue.

Additional Lyrics

3. *Well, I grew up quick and I grew up mean;*
   My fists got hard and my wits got keen.
   Roamed from town to town to hide my shame.
   But I made me a vow to the moon and stars,
   I'd search the honky-tonks and bars,
   And kill that man that give me that awful name.

4. *Well, it was Gatlinburg in mid July,*
   And I had just hit town and my throat was dry.
   I'd thought I'd stop and have myself a brew.
   At an old saloon on a street of mud,
   There at a table dealin' stud,
   Sat the dirty, mangy dog that named me Sue.

5. *Well, I knew that snake was my own sweet dad*
   From a worn-out picture that my mother had.
   And I knew that scar on his cheek and his evil eye.
   He was big and bent and gray and old,
   And I looked at him and my blood ran cold,
   And I said, "My name is Sue. How do you do?
   Now you gonna die." Yeah, that's what I told him.

6. *Well, I hit him hard right between the eyes,*
   And he went down, but to my surprise
   He come up with a knife and cut off a piece of my ear.
   But I busted a chair right across his teeth
   And we crashed through the wall and into the street,
   Kickin' and a-gougin' in the mud and the blood and the beer.

7. *I tell you, I've fought tougher men,*
   But I really can't remember when.
   He kicked like a mule and he bit like a crocodile.
   I heard him laugh and then I heard him cussin'.
   He went for his gun and I pulled mine first.
   He stood there lookin' at me and I saw him smile.

8. *And he said, "Son, this world is rough,*
   And if a man's gonna make it, he's gotta be tough.
   And I know I wouldn't be there to help you along.
   So I gave you that name and I said goodbye.
   I knew you'd have to get tough or die.
   And it's that name that helped to make you strong.

9. *Yeah, he said, "Now, you just fought one helluva fight,*
   And I know you hate me and you've got the right
   To kill me now, and I wouldn't blame you if you do.
   But you ought to thank me before I die
   For the gravel in your guts and the spit in your eye,
   'Cause I'm the son of a bitch that named you Sue."
   Yeah, what could I do? What could I do?

10. *I got all choked up and I threw down my gun*
    Called him my pa and he called me his son.
    And I come away with a different point of view.
    And I think about him now and then,
    Ev'ry time I try and ev'ry time I win.
    And if I ever have a son, I think I'm gonna name him...
    Bill or George. Anything but Sue.
    I still hate that man. Yeah.

Brand New Man

Words and Music by Don Cook, Ronnie Dunn and Kix Brooks

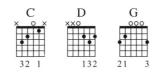

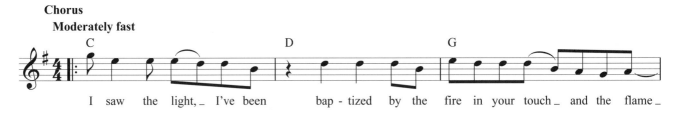

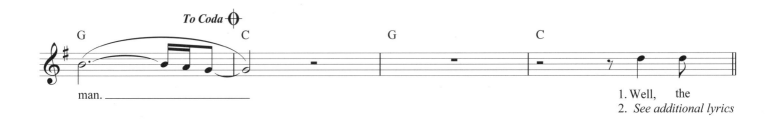

I used to have a wild ___ side, they say a coun-try mile ___ wide. I'd

burn those ___ beer ___ joints ___ down. ___ That's all ___ changed now;

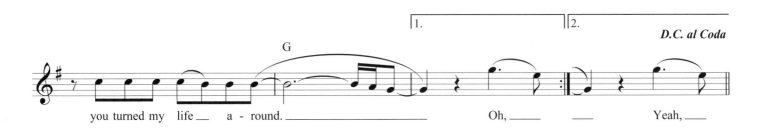

you turned my life ___ a - round. _____ Oh, _____ Yeah, ___

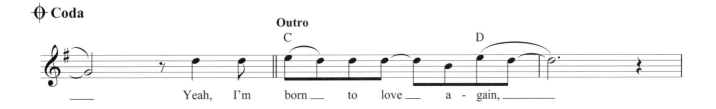

Yeah, I'm born ___ to love ___ a - gain,

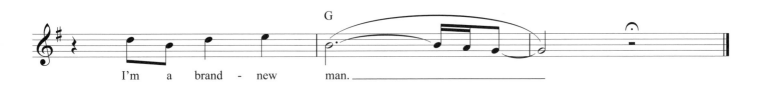

I'm a brand - new man. _____

Additional Lyrics

2. I used to love 'em and leave 'em, oh, I'd brag about my freedom,
   How no one could tie me down.
   Then I met you; now my heart beats true.
   Baby, you and me together feels more like forever
   Than anything I've ever known.
   We're right on track. I ain't lookin' back.

Call Me the Breeze

Words and Music by John Cale

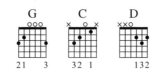

Chorus
Moderately fast

Call / call me the breeze; _ I keep blow - in' down _ the road. _

_ Well, now, they

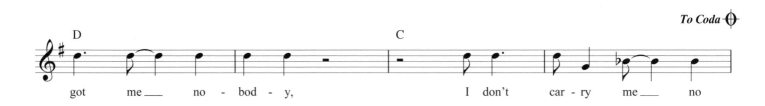

call me the breeze; _ I keep blow - in' down _ the road. _

To Coda

_ I ain't

got me _ no - bod - y, I don't car - ry me _ no

load.   1. Ain't no

Verse

change in the weath - er, ain't no chang - es in me. __
(2., 3.) *See additional lyrics*

__ There ain't no change in the weath -

- er, ain't no chang - es in me. __

And I ain't hid - in' from no - bod - y, no - bod - y's

hid - in' __ from me.   2. Well, I got that
                  3. Well, I

Well, now, they   load. *(Instrumental)*

Additional Lyrics

2. Well, I got that green light, baby; I got to keep movin' on.
 Well, I got that green light, baby; I got to keep movin' on.
 Well, I might go out to California, might go down to Georgia, I don't know.

3. Well, I dig you Georgia peaches; makes me feel right at home.
 Well, now, I dig you Georgia peaches; makes me feel right at home.
 But I don't love me no one woman, so I can't stay in Georgia long.

Cecilia

Words and Music by Paul Simon

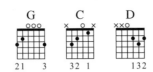

Chorus
Moderately

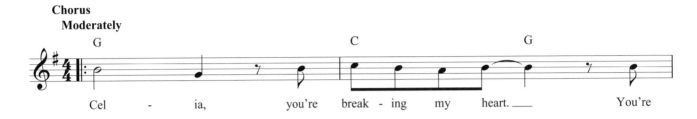

Cel - ia, you're break - ing my heart. ___ You're

shak - ing my con - fi - dence dai - ly. ___ Oh, Ce - cil - ia, I'm

down on my knees. ___ I'm beg - ging you please ___ to come home. ___

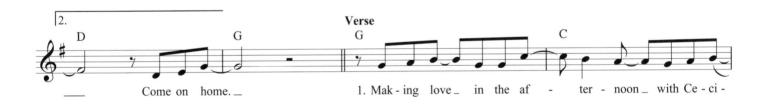

Come on home. ___ 1. Mak - ing love ___ in the af - ter - noon ___ with Ce - ci -

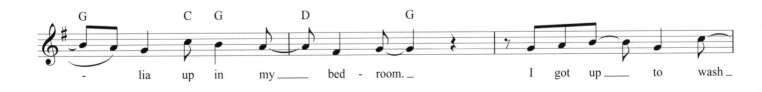

- lia up in my ___ bed - room. ___ I got up ___ to wash

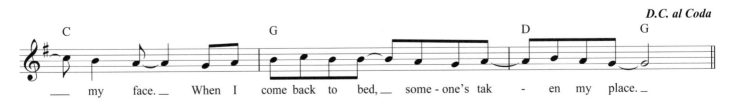

___ my face. ___ When I come back to bed, ___ some - one's tak - en my place. ___

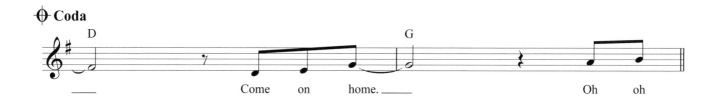

Coda

Come on home. ____ Oh oh

Bridge

oh oh ____ oh oh oh oh oh oh oh oh ____ oh. ____ Ju - bi -

Outro

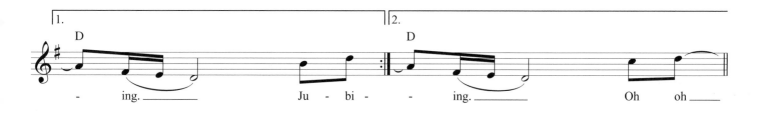

la - tion, she loves me a - gain. __ I fall on the floor __ and I'm laugh -

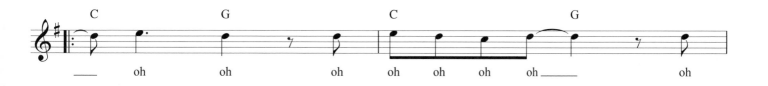

1.
- ing. _____   Ju - bi - 2. - ing. _____ Oh oh ____

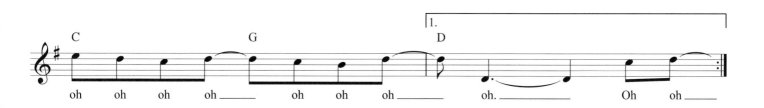

____ oh oh oh oh oh oh oh ____ oh

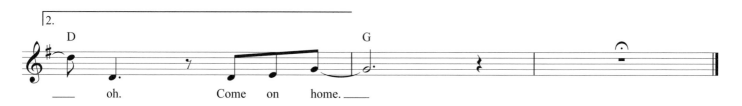

oh oh oh oh ____ oh oh oh ____ oh. ____ 1. Oh oh ____

2.
____ oh. Come on home. ____

Chasing Cars

Words and Music by Gary Lightbody, Tom Simpson, Paul Wilson, Jonathan Quinn and Nathan Connolly

Closer to Free

Words and Music by Sam Llanas and Kurt Neumann

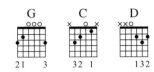

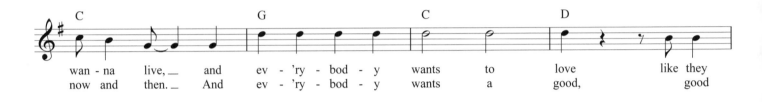

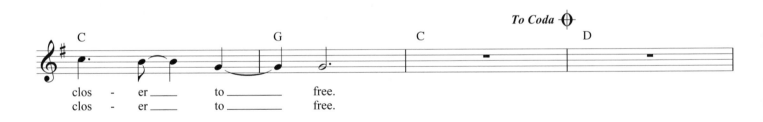

Ev - 'ry - bod - y wants to be

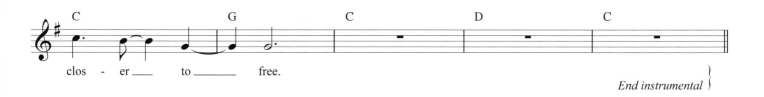

clos - er ____ to _____ free.

End instrumental

Bridge

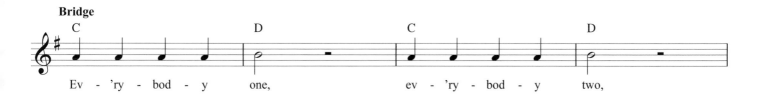

Ev - 'ry - bod - y one, ev - 'ry - bod - y two,

1.   2.   *D.C. al Coda (Lyric 1)*

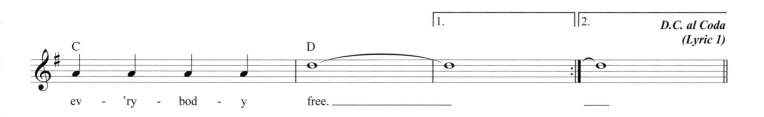

ev - 'ry - bod - y free. _____ ____

Coda

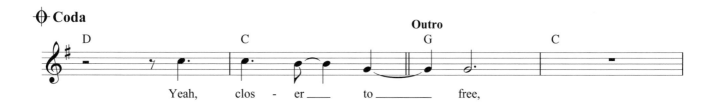

Outro

Yeah, clos - er ____ to _____ free,

yeah, clos - er ____ to free, _____

clos - er ____ to _____ free.

Cold, Cold Heart

Words and Music by Hank Williams

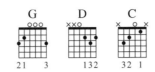

Verse
Moderately, in 2

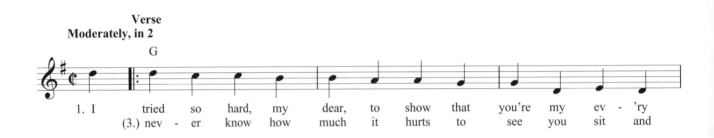

1. I tried so hard, my dear, to show that you're my ev - 'ry
(3.) nev - er know how much it hurts to see you sit and

dream. Yet you're a - fraid each thing I do is just some e - vil
cry. You know you need and want my love, yet you're a - fraid to

scheme. A mem - 'ry from your lone - some past keeps us so far a -
try. Why do you run and hide from life? To try it just ain't

part. Why can't I free your doubt - ful mind and melt your cold, cold
smart. Why can't I free your doubt - ful mind and melt your cold, cold

heart?   2. An - oth - er love be - fore my time made your heart sad and

heart?   4. There was a time when I be - lieved that you be - longed to

blue.   And so my heart is pay - ing now for things I did - n't

me.   But now I know your heart is shack - led to a mem - o -

do.   In an - ger, un - kind words are said that make the tear - drops

ry.   The more I learn to care for you, the more we drift a -

start.   Why can't I free your doubt - ful mind and

part.   Why can't I free your doubt - ful mind and

melt your cold, cold heart?   3. You'll melt your cold, cold heart?

Dizzy Miss Lizzie

Words and Music by Larry Williams

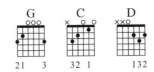

% Intro

(Instrumental)

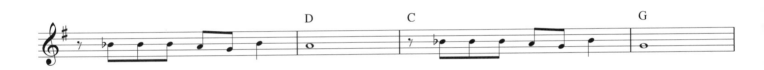

Verse

1. You make me diz-zy, Miss __ Liz - zie, the way you rock and roll. __
2., 3. *See additional lyrics*

__ You make me diz-zy, Miss __ Liz - zie,

when you do the Stroll. _____ Come on, Miss Liz - zie,

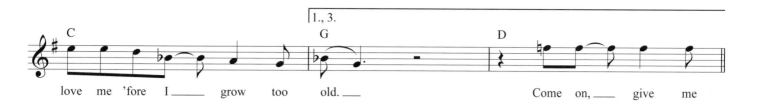
love me 'fore I_____ grow too old._____   Come on,_____ give me

Chorus

fe - ver,   put your lit - tle hand in mine._____

You make me diz - zy, diz - zy, Liz - zie.   Ooh, girl, you look so

fine._____   Just a - rock - in' and a - roll - in',_____

To Coda ⊕

girl, I said I wish you were mine._____   *(Instrumental)*

D.S. al Coda
(take 1st ending)   ⊕ **Coda**

man. __   *(Instrumental)*

Additional Lyrics

2. You make me dizzy, Miss Lizzie,
   When you call my name.
   Woo, baby, say you're driving me insane.
   Come on, come on, come on, come on, baby,
   I wanna be your lovin' man.

3. Run and tell your mama
   I want you to be my bride.
   Run and tell your brother.
   Baby, don't run and hide.
   You make me dizzy, Miss Lizzie.
   Girl, I wanna marry you.

35

Early Mornin' Rain

Words and Music by Gordon Lightfoot

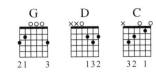

Verse

Moderately bright, in 2

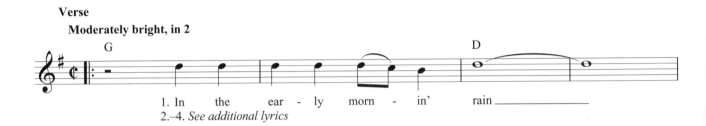

1. In the ear - ly morn - in' rain _____
2.–4. *See additional lyrics*

with a dol - lar in ____ my hand, _____

with an ach - in' in my heart _____

and my pock - ets full of sand, _____

I'm a long way from home, _____

and   I   miss   my   loved   ones   so. _____

In   the   ear - ly   morn - in'   rain, _____

with   no   place   to   go. _____

1.–3.   4.

Additional Lyrics

2. Out on runway number nine,
   Big 707 set to go.
   But I'm stuck here in the grass
   Where the cold wind blows.
   Now the liquor tasted good,
   And the women all were fast.
   Well, there she goes, my friend,
   She's rollin' now at last.

3. Hear the mighty engines roar,
   See the silver bird on high.
   She's away and westward bound,
   Far above the clouds she'll fly,
   Where the mornin' rain don't fall
   And the sun always shines.
   She'll be flyin' o'er my home
   In about three hours' time.

4. This old airport's got me down;
   It's no earthly good to me.
   'Cause I'm stuck here on the ground,
   As cold and drunk as I can be.
   You can't jump a jet plane
   Like you can a freight train,
   So I'd best be on my way
   In the early mornin' rain.

The First Cut Is the Deepest

Words and Music by Cat Stevens

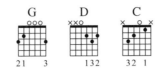

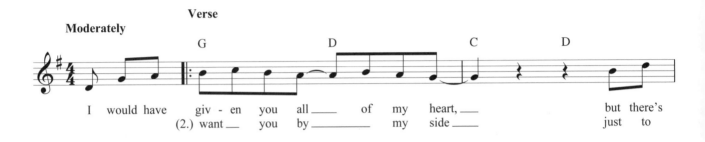

I would have giv - en you all ____ of my heart, ____ but there's
(2.) want ____ you by ____ my side ____ just to

some - one who's torn it a - part. ____ And she's
help me dry the tears that I've cried. ____ And I'm

tak - en just all ____ that I had, ____ but } if you want, I'll ____
sure gon - na give you a try, ____ and }

try ____ to love a - gain. Ba - by, I'll try ____

to love a - gain, but I know: _____

Chorus

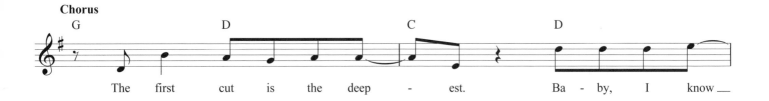

The first cut is the deep - est. Ba - by, I know _____

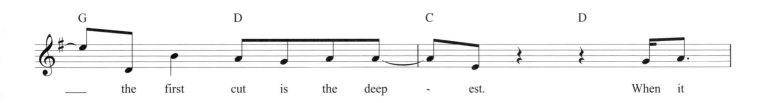

_____ the first cut is the deep - est. When it

comes to be - in' luck - y, she's cursed. _____ When it

1.

comes to lov - in' me, she's worst. _____ 2. I still

2.

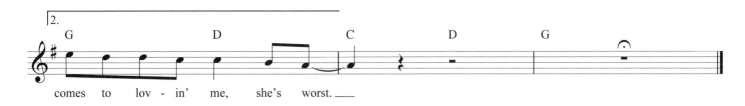

comes to lov - in' me, she's worst. _____

Games People Play

Words and Music by Joe South

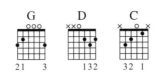

Moderately slow, in 2

1. Oh, the games peo-ple play, now, ev-'ry night and ev-'ry day, now,
(2.–4.) See additional lyrics

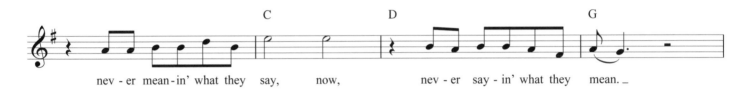

nev-er mean-in' what they say, now, nev-er say-in' what they mean. —

While they while a-way the ho-urs in their i-vo-ry tow-ers,

'til they're cov-ered up with flow-ers, in the back of a black lim-ou-

sine.   La, da, da, da, da, da, da.   La, da, da, da, da,

da,   da, dee.   Talk-in' 'bout you and me, and the games peo-ple

play, now.   2. Oh, we make one an-   Oh,
4. Look a-round, tell me

Bridge

yeah, _____ ooh, ooh. _____ Oh,

yeah. _____ Come on, _____ come on, come on, come on.

Whoa, _ whoa, _ oh, _____ oh. __

D.S. al Coda (with repeat)

Coda

__ 3. Peo - ple walk - in' up La, da, da, da,

Outro-Chorus

da, da, da. La, da, da, da, da, da, da, dee. Talk - in' 'bout

Repeat and fade

you and me, and the games peo - ple play, now. La, da, da, da,

Additional Lyrics

2. Oh, we make one another cry, break a heart then we say goodbye,
   Cross our hearts and we hope to die, that the other was to blame.
   Neither one will ever give in. So we gaze at an eight-by-ten,
   Thinkin' 'bout the things that might have been, and it's a dirty rotten shame.

3. People walkin' up to you, singin', "Glory, hallelujah!"
   And they're tryin' to sock it to you in the name of the Lord.
   They gonna teach you how to meditate, read your horoscope, cheat your fate,
   And, furthermore, to hell with hate. Come on, get on board.

4. Look around, tell me what you see. What's happenin' to you and me?
   God, grant me the serenity to just remember who I am,
   'Cause you're givin' up your sanity for your pride and your vanity.
   Turn your back on humanity, oh, and you don't give a (da, da, da, da, da...)

The Green Door

Words and Music by Bob Davie and Marvin Moore

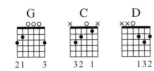

Verse
Moderately, in 2

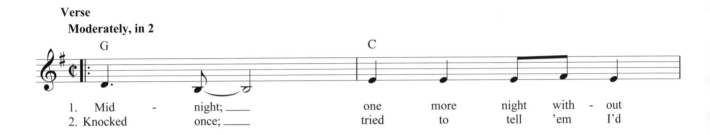

1. Mid - night; ____ one more night with - out
2. Knocked once; ____ tried to tell 'em I'd

sleep - in'. ____ Watch - ing ____
been there. ____ Door slammed; ____

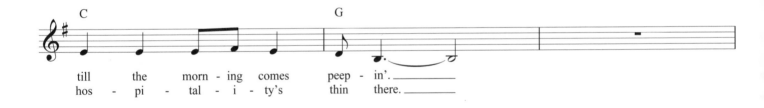

till the morn - ing comes peep - in'. ____
hos - pi - tal - i - ty's thin there. ____

Green door, ____ what's the se - cret you're keep - in'? ____
Won - der ____ just what's go - in' on in there. ____

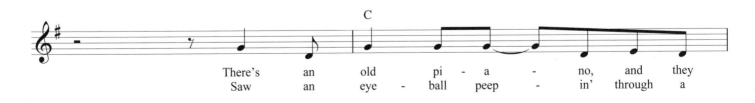

There's an old pi - a - no, and they
Saw an eye - ball peep - in' through a

play it hot____ be - hind the green door.____
smok - y cloud____ be - hind the green door.____

Chorus

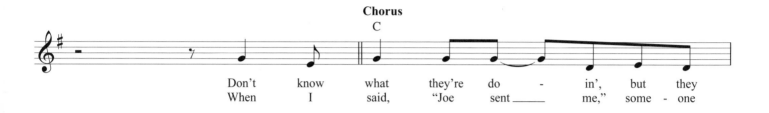

Don't know what they're do - in', but they
When I said, "Joe sent____ me," some - one

laugh a lot____ be - hind the green door.____
laughed out loud____ be - hind the green door.____

Wish they'd let me in____ so I could
All I want to do____ is join the

1.

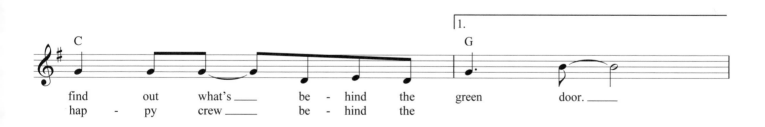

find out what's____ be - hind the green door.____
hap - py crew____ be - hind the

2.

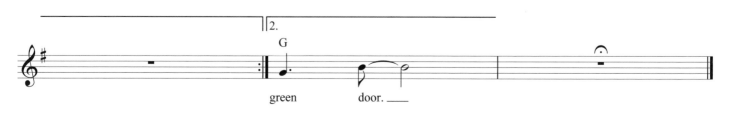

green door.____

He Stopped Loving Her Today

Words and Music by Bobby Braddock and Curly Putman

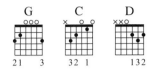

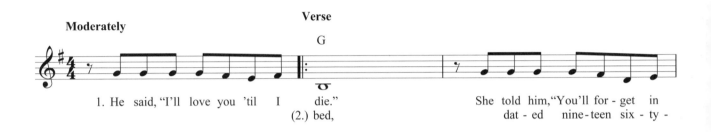

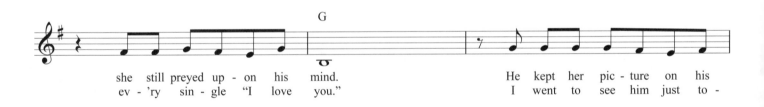

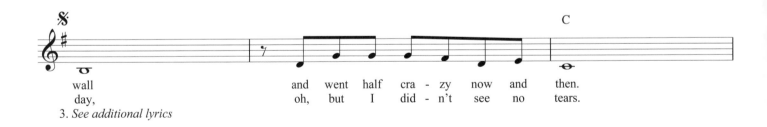

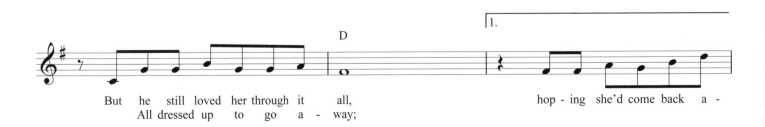

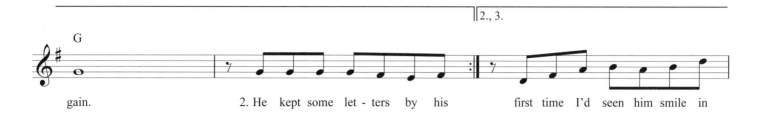

gain.   2. He kept some let - ters by his   first time I'd seen him smile in

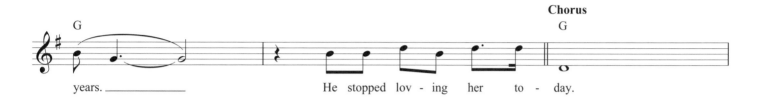

years. _____ He stopped lov - ing her to - day.

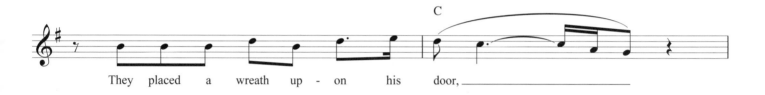

They placed a wreath up - on his door, _____

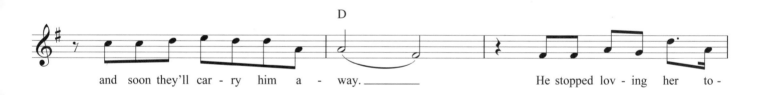

and soon they'll car - ry him a - way. _____ He stopped lov - ing her to -

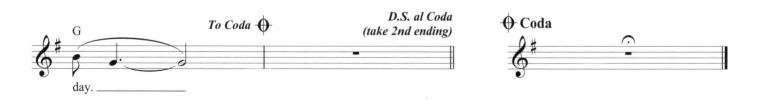

day. _____

Additional Lyrics

3. *(Spoken:)* *You know, she came to see him one last time.*
We all wondered if she would.
And it came running through my mind:
This time he's over her for good.

Here's a Quarter
(Call Someone Who Cares)

Words and Music by Travis Tritt

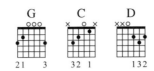

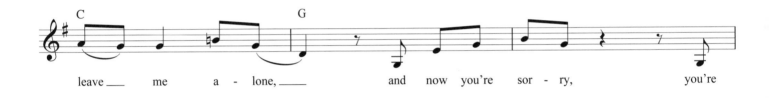

1. You say you were wrong to ev - er
(2.) *See additional lyrics*

leave ___ me a - lone, ___ and now you're sor - ry, you're

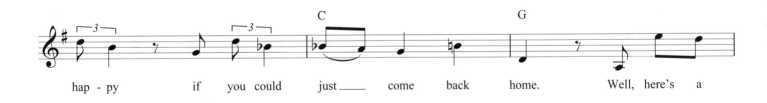

lone - some ___ and scared. ___ And you say you'd be

happy if you could just ___ come back home. Well, here's a

quar - ter. ___ Call some - one ___ who cares. ___ Call

Chorus

some - one who'll _ lis - ten and might give a ____ damn; _ may - be

one of ____ your sor - did af - fairs. ____ But don't you

come a - round here ____ hand - in' ____ me none of ____ your lines. ____

_ Here's a quar - ter. ____ Call some - one __ who cares. ____

2. Girl, I Yeah, here's a quar - ter. Call _ some - one __ who cares. _

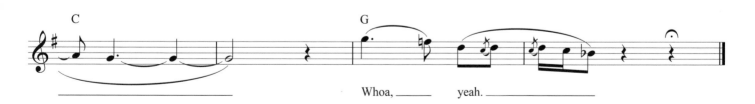

____ Whoa, ____ yeah. ____

Additional Lyrics

2. Girl, I thought what we had could never turn bad,
So your leaving caught me unaware.
But the fact is you've run, girl; that can't be undone.
So, here's a quarter. Call someone who cares.

Hold My Hand

Words and Music by Darius Carlos Rucker, Everett Dean Felber, Mark William Bryan and James George Sonefeld

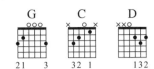

Moderately

𝄋 Verse

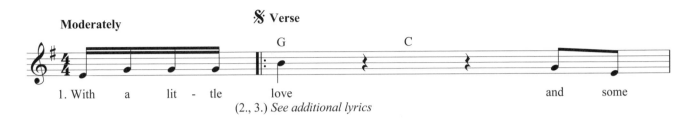

1. With a lit - tle love
(2., 3.) *See additional lyrics*
and some

ten - der - ness, ___ we'll walk up - on ___ the wa - ter. We'll

rise a - bove ___ the mess. ___ With a lit - tle peace ___ and some

har - mo - ny, ___ we'll take the world ___ to - geth - er. We'll

Pre-Chorus

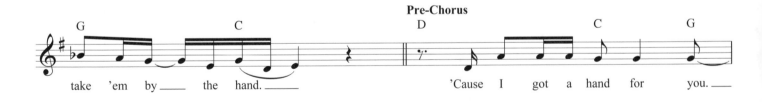

take 'em by ___ the hand. ___ 'Cause I got a hand for you. ___

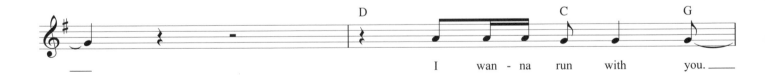

___ I wan - na run with you. ___

___ 2. Yes - ter - ___ Won't you let me run ___ with you? ___

Additional Lyrics

2. Yesterday I saw you standing there.
   Your head was down, your eyes were red,
   No comb had touched your hair.
   I said, "Get up and let me see you smile.
   We'll take a walk together.
   Walk the road a while."

3. See, I was wasted, and I was wasting time
   'Til I thought about your problems,
   I thought about your crime.
   Then I stood up and I screamed aloud,
   "I don't wanna be part of your problems,
   Don't wanna be part of your crowd."

Honeycomb

Words and Music by Bob Merrill

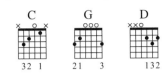

Chorus
Moderately, in 2

Hon - ey - comb, won't - cha be my ba - by? Hon - ey - comb, be my

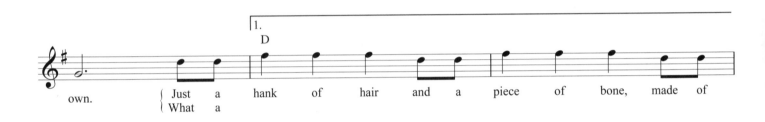

own. Just a hank of hair and a piece of bone, made of
What a

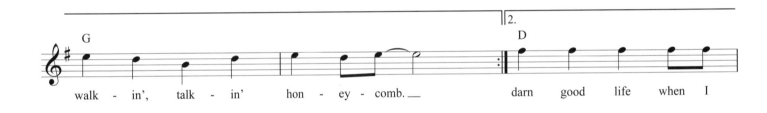

walk - in', talk - in' hon - ey - comb. — darn good life when I

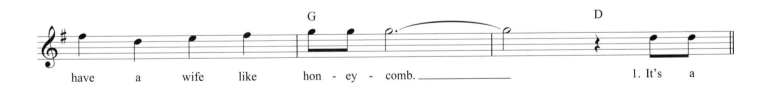

have a wife like hon - ey - comb. _____ 1. It's a

Verse

darn good life, and it's kind of fun - ny how the
(2.) combed the world and they gath - ered all _____ of the

C

bee was made and the bee made hon - ey. And the
hon - ey - comb in one made sweet ball. And the

D

hon - ey - bee, look - in' for a home,
hon - ey - comb from a mil - lion home trips

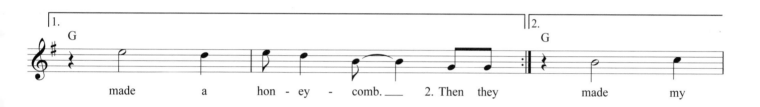

1.   G

made a hon - ey - comb. 2. Then they

2.   G

made my

Outro-Chorus

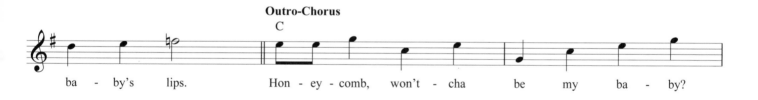

C

ba - by's lips. Hon - ey - comb, won't - cha be my ba - by?

G   D

Hon - ey - comb, be my own. What a darn good life when I

G

have a wife like hon - ey - comb.

I Fall to Pieces

Words and Music by Hank Cochran and Harlan Howard

Little Honda

Words and Music by Brian Wilson and Mike Love

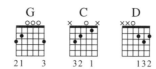

Verse

Moderately fast

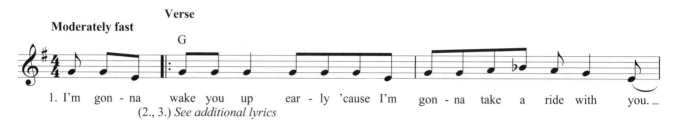

1. I'm gon - na wake you up ear - ly 'cause I'm gon - na take a ride with you. _
(2., 3.) *See additional lyrics*

We're go - ing down to the Hon - da shop, I'll

tell you what we're gon - na do. __ Put on a rag - ged sweat - shirt, I'll take you

an - y - where you want me to. __ First gear, it's all right. _

__ Sec - ond gear, __ a lean right. __ Third gear, __ hang on tight. _

__ Fast - er, ___ it's all right. 2. It's not a right. First
3. It climbs the

Additional Lyrics

2. It's not a big motorcycle, just a groovy little motor bike.
   It's more fun than a barrel of monkeys, that two-wheeled bike.
   We'll ride on out of the town to anyplace I know you like.

3. It climbs the hills like a Matchless 'cause my Honda's built really light.
   When I go into the turns, tilt with me and hang on tight.
   I'd better turn on the lights so we can ride my Honda tonight.

I Got You
(I Feel Good)

Words and Music by James Brown

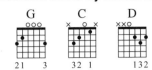

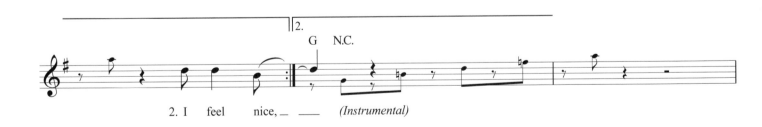

Bridge

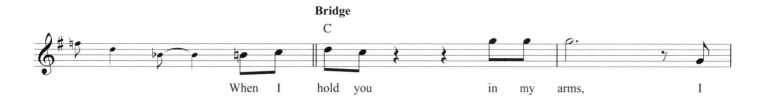

When I hold you in my arms, I

know that I can't do no wrong; _____ and when I hold __ you in my

D.S. al Coda
(Lyric 1)

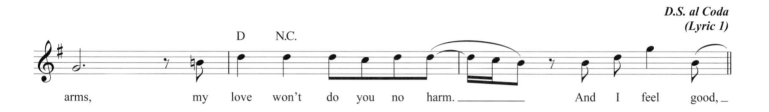

arms, my love won't do you no harm. _____ And I feel good, __

Coda

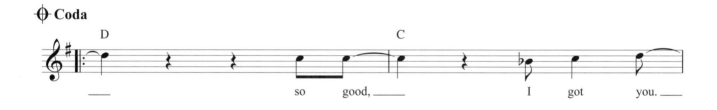

__ so good, _____ I got you. __

__ *(Instrumental)* So good, __

Hey!

I Still Haven't Found What I'm Looking For

Words and Music by U2

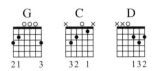

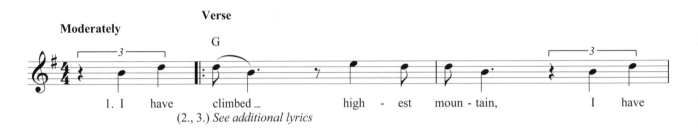

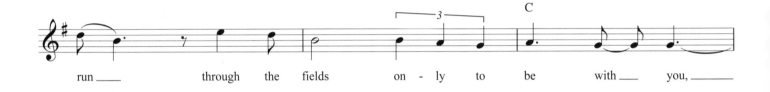

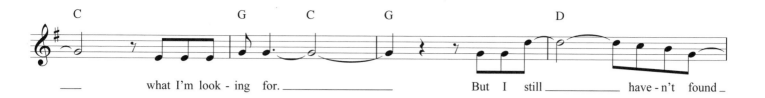

___ what I'm look - ing for. _____ But I still _____ have - n't found _

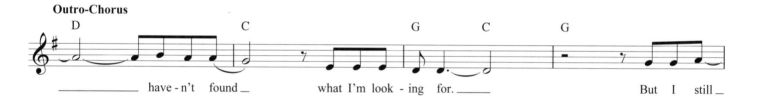

___ what I'm look - ing for. _____ 2. I have ___ But I still _
3. I be -

Outro-Chorus

_____ have - n't found _ what I'm look - ing for. _____ But I still _

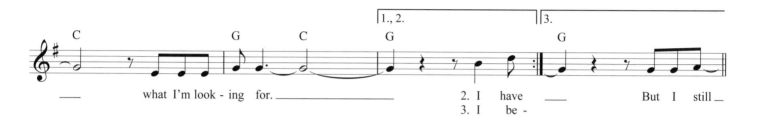

_____ have - n't found _ what I'm look - ing for. _____

Additional Lyrics

2. I have kissed honey lips, felt the healing fingertips.
   It burned like fire, this burning desire.
   I have spoke with the tongue of angels, I have held the hand of the devil.
   It was warm in the night, I was cold as a stone.

3. I believe in the kingdom come, then all the colors will bleed into one,
   Bleed into one. But, yes, I'm still runnin'.
   You broke the bonds and you loosed the chains, carried the cross of my shame,
   Of my shame. You know I believe it.

If I Were a Carpenter

Words and Music by Tim Hardin

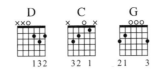

Verse
Moderately, in 2

1. *Male:* If I _____ were a car-pen-ter, and you were a
2. *See additional lyrics*

la - dy, would you mar-ry me an-y-way?

Would you have my ba - by? _____ *Female:* If you _____ were a

car - pen - ter, and I were a la - dy,

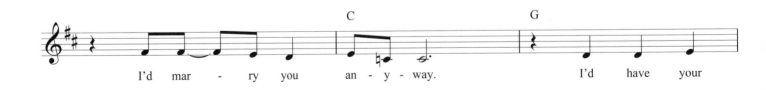

I'd mar - ry you an - y - way. I'd have your

ba - by. _____ *Male:* If a tin - ker was my trade, _____

would I _____ still find you? *Female:* I'd be car - ry - in' the

pots you made, fol - low - ing be - hind _____ you. _____

Chorus

_____ *Both:* Save your love through lone - li - ness, _____

save your love through sor - row. _____ I gave you my

on - li - ness; _____ give me your to - mor - row.

Additional Lyrics

2. *Male:* If I were a miller at a mill wheel grindin',
   Would you miss your colored blouse and your soft shoes shinin'?

Female: If you were a miller at a mill wheel grindin',
    I'd not miss my colored blouse and my soft shoes shinin'.

 Male: If I worked my hands in wood, would you still love me?
Female: I'd answer you, "Yes, I would. *Male:* And would you not be above me...

 Male: ...If I were a carpenter, and you were a lady?
Female: I'd marry you anyway. I'd have your baby.

It's Hard to Be Humble

Words and Music by Mac Davis

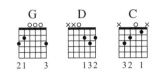

Oh, Lord, it's hard __ to be hum - ble when you're per - fect in

ev - er - y way. __ I can't wait __ to look in __ the mir - ror

'cause I get bet - ter look - in' each __ day. __ To

know me is to love me, I must be a

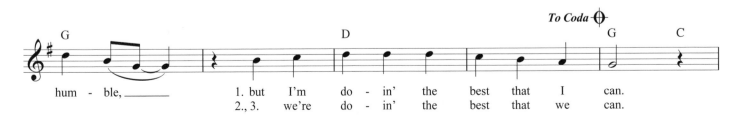

hell of a man. __ Oh, Lord, it's hard __ to be

hum - ble, __ 1. but I'm do - in' the best that I can.
2., 3. we're do - in' the best that we can.

Verse

1. I used ____ to have a girl - friend, but I guess she just

2. *See additional lyrics*

could-n't com - pete with all ____ of these love - starved _ wom - en

who keep clam-or - ing ____ at my ____ feet. Well, I prob - 'ly could

find me an - oth - er, but I guess they're all ____ in awe ____ of

me. Who cares? _ I nev - er get lone - some ____ 'cause I

2nd time, D.S. al Coda   **Coda**

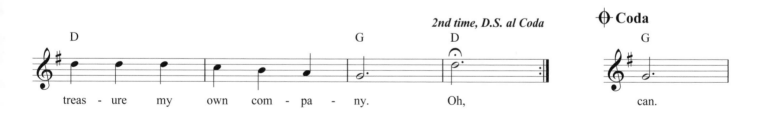

treas - ure my own com - pa - ny. Oh, can.

Outro

We're do - in' the best that we can. ____

Additional Lyrics

2. I guess you could say I'm a loner, a cowboy outlaw, tough and proud.
   Oh, I could have lots of friends if I wanna, but then I wouldn't stand out from the crowd.
   Some folks say that I'm egotistical. Hell, I don't even know what that means.
   I guess it has something to do with the way that I fill out my skin-tight blue jeans.

The Joker

Words and Music by Steve Miller, Eddie Curtis and Ahmet Ertegun

I sure don't want to hurt no one. _____ I'm a
I get my lov - ing on the run. _____ Ooh, hoo. _____

_____ Ooh, hoo. _____

Guitar Solo

Verse

3. You're the cut - est thing that I ev - er did see. _____ I real - ly love your peach - es, want to

shake your tree. _____ Love - y dove - y, love - y dove - y, love - y dove - y all the time. _____

Ooh, wee, ba - by, I'll sure show you a good time. _____ 'Cause I'm a

Outro-Chorus

pick - er, I'm a grin - ner, I'm a lov - er, and I'm a sin - ner.

I play my mu - sic in the sun. _____ I'm a jok - er, I'm a smok - er, I'm a

Repeat and fade

mid - night tok - er.   I get my lov - in' on the run. _____   I'm a
                         I sure don't wan - na hurt no one. _____

King of the Road

Words and Music by Roger Miller

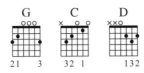

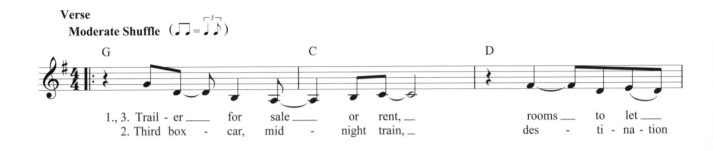

Verse
Moderate Shuffle

1., 3. Trail - er ___ for sale ___ or rent, ___ rooms ___ to let ___
2. Third box - car, mid - night train, ___ des - ti - na - tion

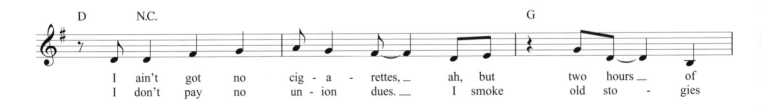

fif - ty cents. ___ No phone, ___ no pool, ___ no pets. ___
Ban - gor, Maine. ___ Old worn - out suit ___ and shoes, ___

I ain't got no cig - a - rettes, ___ ah, but two hours ___ of
I don't pay no un - ion dues. ___ I smoke old sto - gies

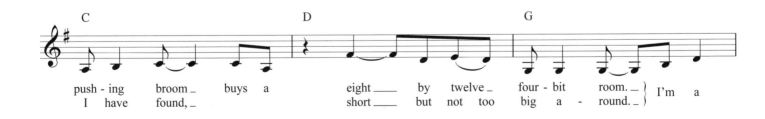

push - ing broom ___ buys a eight ___ by twelve ___ four - bit room. ___ } I'm a
I have found, ___ short ___ but not too big a - round. ___ }

man   of   means ___   by   no   means,   king   of   the   road. _

1.

2.

Bridge

___   ___   I   know   ev - er - y   en - gi - neer   on

ev - er - y   train, __   all   of   the   chil - dren   and   all   of   their   names,   and

ev - er - y   hand - out   in   ev - er - y   town   and   ev - 'ry   lock   that   ain't   locked   when

⊕ **Coda**

D.C. al Coda
(Lyric 1)

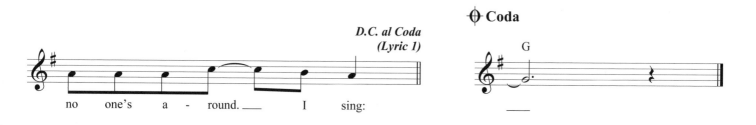

no   one's   a - round. ___   I   sing: ___

Mean Woman Blues

Words and Music by Claude DeMetruis

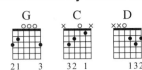

Chorus
Moderate Rock

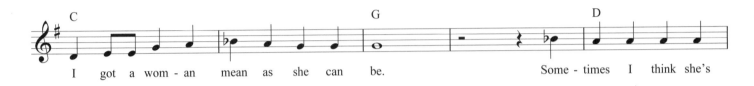

I got a wom-an mean as she can be.

I got a wom-an mean as she can be. Some-times I think she's

al-most mean as me. 1. A black cat up and died of fright
(2.–4.) *See additional lyrics*

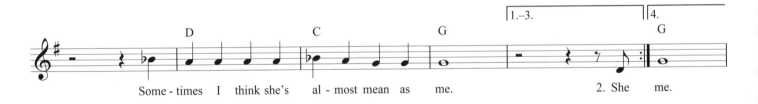

'cause she crossed his path last night. Oh, I got a wom-an mean as she can be.

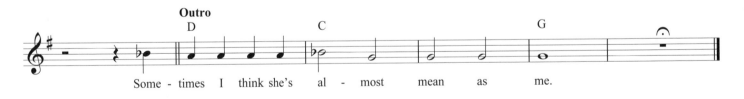

Some-times I think she's al-most mean as me. 2. She me.

Outro

Some-times I think she's al-most mean as me.

Additional Lyrics

2. She kiss so hard she bruise my lips.
   Hurts so good my heart just flips.
   Oh, I got a woman mean as she can be.
   Sometimes I think she's almost mean as me.

3. The strangest gal I ever had;
   Never happy 'less she's mad.
   Oh, I got a woman mean as she can be.
   Sometimes I think she's almost mean as me.

4. She makes love without a smile.
   Ooh, hot dog, that drives me wild.
   Oh, I got a woman mean as she can be.
   Sometimes I think she's almost mean as me.

Oh Boy!

Words and Music by Sunny West, Bill Tilghman and Norman Petty

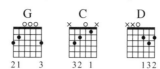

Verse
Brightly, in 2

1., 3. All of my love, all of my kiss - in', you don't know what
2. All of my life I been wait - in', to - night there'll be no

Chorus

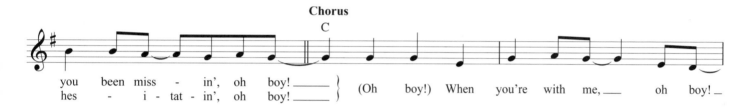

you been miss - in', oh boy! ____ } (Oh boy!) When you're with me, ___ oh boy! __
hes - i - tat - in', oh boy! ____

To Coda

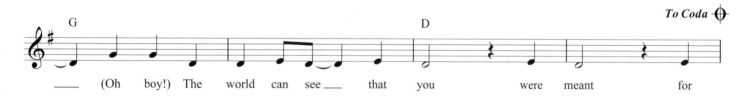

__ (Oh boy!) The world can see __ that you were meant for

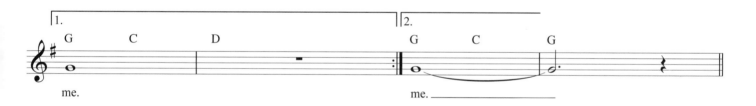

1.
me.

2.
me. ____

Bridge

Stars ap - pear and shad - ows fall - in', you can hear my ___

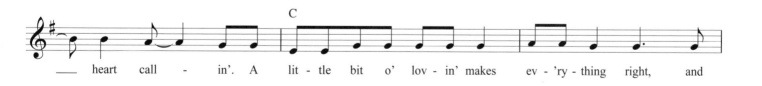

___ heart call - in'. A lit - tle bit o' lov - in' makes ev - 'ry - thing right, and

D.C. al Coda

I'm gon - na see my ba - by to - night! ____

Coda

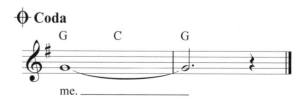

me. ____

The Night's Too Long

Words and Music by Lucinda Williams

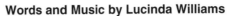

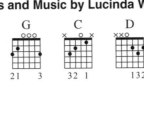

Verse
Moderately fast

1. Syl - vi - a was work - in' ___ as a wait - ress in Beau-
(3.) *See additional lyrics*

- mont. She said, "I'm mov - in' a - way, ___ I'm gon - na

get what I want. ___ I'm tired ___ of these small -

- town boys; ___ they don't move fast e - nough. ___ I'm gon - na

find me one ___ who wears a leath - er jack - et and like his ___ liv - in' rough."

Verse

2. So, she saved ___ her tips and o - ver - time ___ and
4. *See additional lyrics*

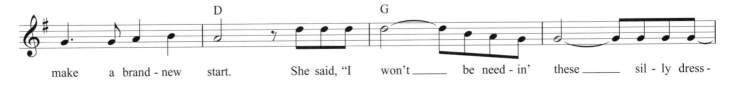

bought an old, rust - y car. ___ She sold most ___ ev - 'ry - thing ___ she had ___ to

make a brand - new start. She said, "I won't ___ be need - in' these ___ sil - ly dress-

-es and ny-lon hose, ___ 'cause when I ___ get to where I'm go-

-in', I'm gon-na buy me all ___ new clothes." ___ The night's ___ too

Chorus

long; _____ it just drags on ___ and on. ___

And then there's nev-er e-nough; ___ that's when the sun starts com-in' up, ___

Don't let go of her hand; _____ you just might be the right ___

man. ___ She loves the night, ___ she loves ___ the night. ___ She

does-n't want the night, ___ don't want it to end, don't want it to

1.
end. 3. Well, she

2.
Don't want it to end.

Additional Lyrics

3. Well, she works in an office now,
   And she guesses the pay's all right.
   She can buy a few new things to wear
   And still go out at night.
   And as soon as she gets home from work,
   She wants to be out with the crowd,
   Where she can dance and toss her head back
   And laugh out loud.

4. Well, the music's playin' fast
   And they just met.
   He presses up against her
   And his shirt's all soaked with sweat.
   And with her back against the bar,
   She can listen to the band.
   And she's holdin' a Corona
   And it's cold against her hand.

No Particular Place to Go

Words and Music by Chuck Berry

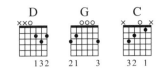

Intro
Moderately

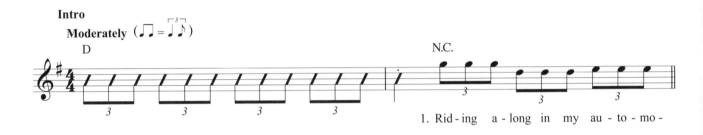

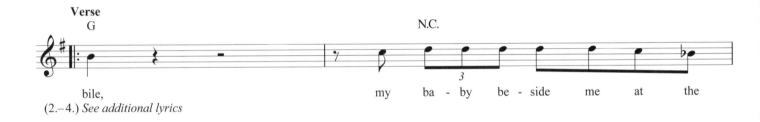

1. Rid - ing a - long in my au - to - mo -

Verse

bile,
(2.–4.) *See additional lyrics*

my ba - by be - side me at the

wheel,

I stole a kiss at the turn of a

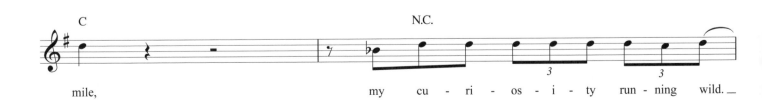

mile,

my cu - ri - os - i - ty run - ning wild. _

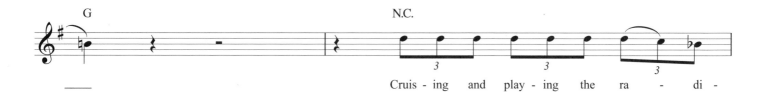

Cruis - ing and play - ing the ra - di -

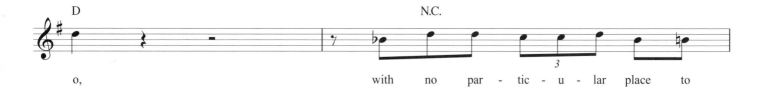

o, with no par - tic - u - lar place to

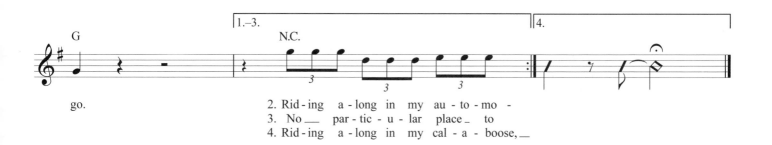

go.

2. Rid - ing a - long in my au - to - mo -
3. No __ par - tic - u - lar place __ to
4. Rid - ing a - long in my cal - a - boose, __

Additional Lyrics

2. Riding along in my automobile,
   I was anxious to tell her the way I feel.
   So I told her softly and sincere,
   And she leaned and whispered in my ear
   Cuddlin' more and driving slow,
   With no particular place to go.

3. No particular place to go,
   So we parked way out on the cocamo.
   The night was young and the moon was gold,
   So we both decided to take a stroll.
   Can you imagine the way I felt?
   I couldn't unfasten her safety belt.

4. Riding along in my calaboose,
   Still trying to get her belt aloose.
   All the way home I held a grudge
   For the safety belt that wouldn't budge.
   Cruising and playing the radio,
   With no particular place to go.

One Bourbon, One Scotch, One Beer

Words and Music by John Lee Hooker

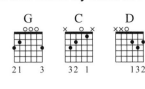

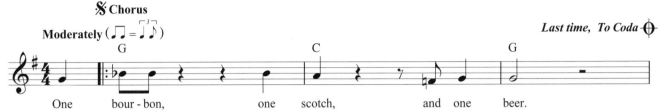

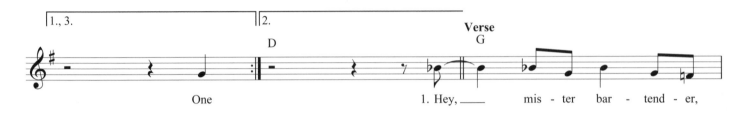

Release Me

Words and Music by Robert Yount, Eddie Miller and Dub Williams

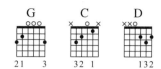

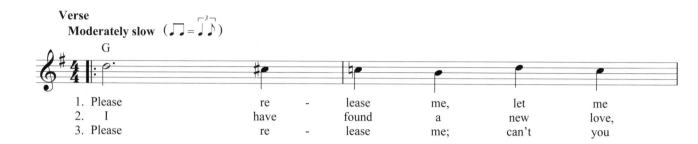

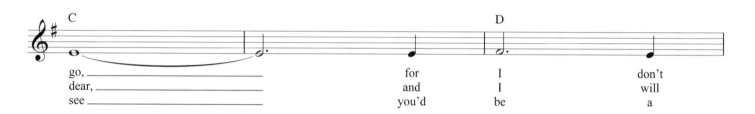

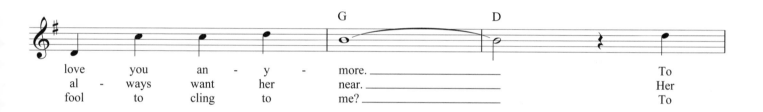

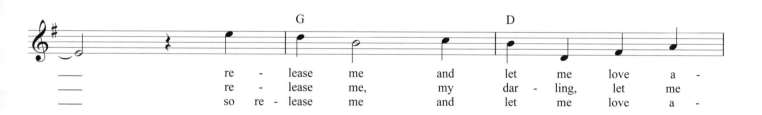

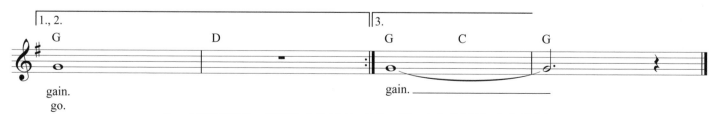

Ring of Fire

Words and Music by Merle Kilgore and June Carter

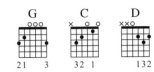

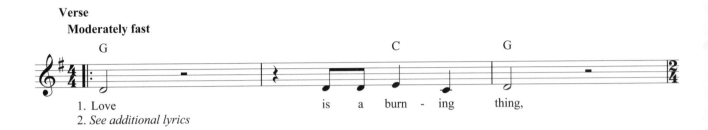

Verse
Moderately fast

1. Love ... is a burn - ing thing,

2. *See additional lyrics*

and it makes

a fier - y ring.

Bound ... by wild __ de - sire, __

I fell in - to a

ring of _____ fire.   I   fell

in - to   a   burn - in'   ring   of   fi - re.   I   went

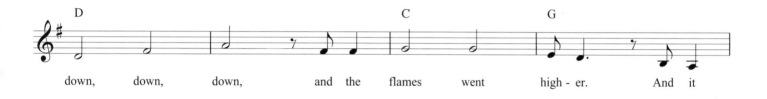

down,   down,   down,   and the   flames   went   high - er.   And it

burns,   burns,   burns,   the   ring _____   of   fi - re,

the   ring   of   fire.   2. The

Additional Lyrics

2. The taste of love is sweet
   When hearts like ours meet.
   I fell for you like a child,
   Oh, but the fire went wild.

Ruby Baby

Words and Music by Jerry Leiber and Mike Stoller

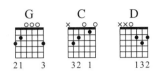

Verse
Moderately bright

1. I love a girl and - a Ru - by is her name. ___
2. Each time I see you, ___ ba - by, my heart cries. ___

This girl don't ___ love me, but I love her just the same. ___
Tell ya, I'm gon - na steal ___ you a - way from all those guys. ___

Whoa, _____ Ru - by, Ru - by, how I want ya, like a ghost I'm - a
Whoa, _____ from the hap - py day I met ya, I made a bet that I was

gon - na haunt ya. Ru - by, Ru - by, Ru - by, will you be
going to get ya. Ru - by, Ru - by, Ru - by, will you be

Chorus

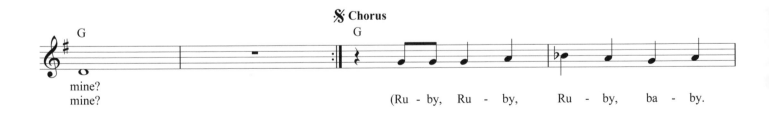

mine?
mine?   (Ru - by, Ru - by, Ru - by, ba - by.

Ru - by, Ru - by, Ru - by, ba - by.   Ru - by, Ru - by,

Ru - by, ba - by. Ru - by, Ru - by, Ru - by, ba - by.

Verse
To Coda

Ah, _____ Ru - by, Ru - by, Ru - by, ba - by.) 3. I love this girl; I said - a,

Ru - by is her name. ___ When this girl looks at me, she just

sets my soul a - flame. ___ Whoa, _____ got some hugs and - a

kiss - es too, yeah, and I'm gon - na give them - a all to you. Now lis - ten:

D.S. al Coda

Ru - by, Ru - by, when will you be mine?

⊕ **Coda**
Outro

Ru - by, Ru - by, when will you be mine? _____

Seven Bridges Road

Words and Music by Stephen T. Young

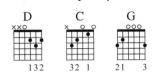

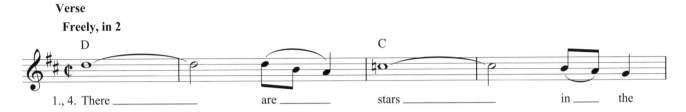

1., 4. There _____ are _____ stars _____ in the

south - ern sky. And if

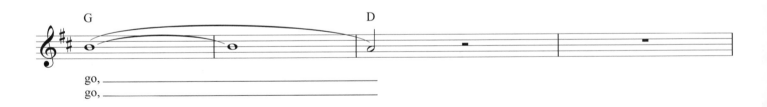

South - ward _____ as _____ you _____
ev - er _____ you de - cide _____ you should

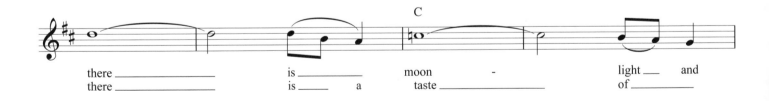

go, _____
go, _____

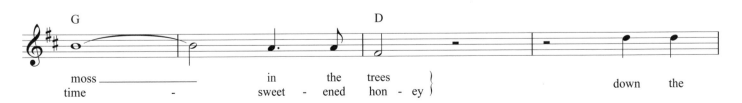

there _____ is _____ moon - light _____ and
there _____ is a taste _____ of _____

moss _____ in the trees
time - sweet - ened hon - ey down the

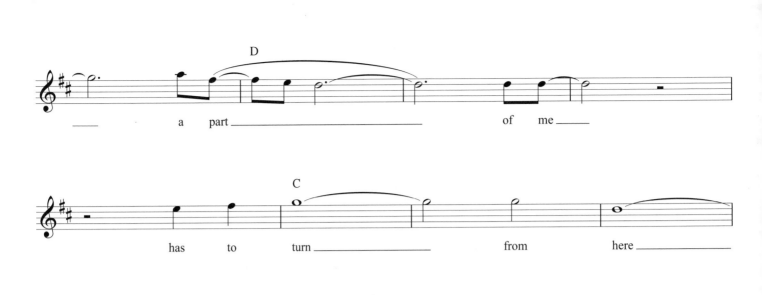

a part _____ of me _____

has to turn _____ from here _____

and go,

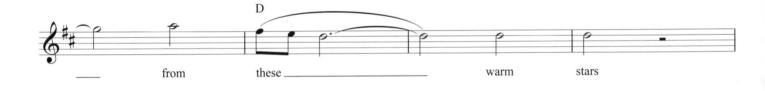

run - ning _____ like a child _____

from these _____ warm stars

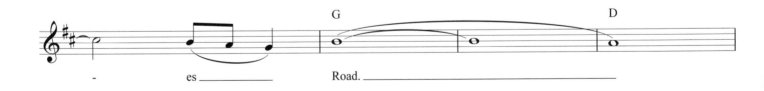

down the Sev - en _____ Bridg -

- es _____ Road. _____

D.C. al Coda

Coda

Steal My Kisses

Words and Music by Ben Harper

Verse
Moderate groove

1. I pulled in to Nash-ville, Ten-nes-see, but
2., 3. *See additional lyrics*

you would-n't e-ven come a-round to see me. And

since you're head-ing up to Car-o-li-na, you

know I'm gon-na be right there be-hind ya. 'Cause I

Chorus

al-ways have to steal my kiss-es from you. I

al-ways have to steal my kiss-es from you.

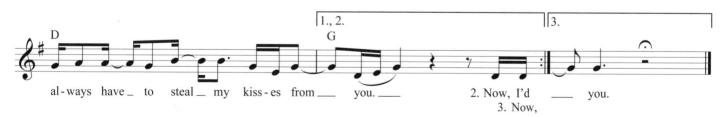

Al-ways have to steal my kiss-es from you. I

al-ways have to steal my kiss-es from you. 2. Now, I'd you.
3. Now,

Additional Lyrics

2. Now, I'd love to feel that warm southern rain.
   Just to hear it fall is the sweetest sounding thing.
   And to see it fall on your simple country dress,
   It's like heaven to me, I must confess.

3. Now, I've been hanging 'round you for days,
   But when I lean in, you just turn your head away.
   Whoa, no, you didn't mean that.
   She said, "I love the way you think, but I hate the way you act."

Shelter from the Storm

Words and Music by Bob Dylan

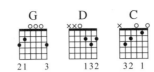

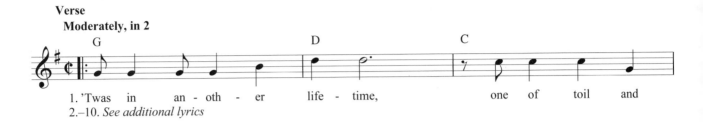

Verse
Moderately, in 2

1. 'Twas in an-oth-er life-time, one of toil and
2.–10. *See additional lyrics*

blood, when black-ness was a vir-tue and the

road was full of mud. _____ I came in from the

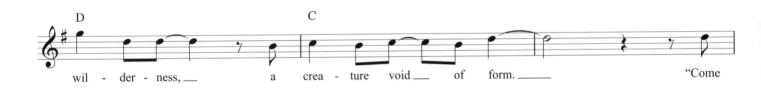

wil-der-ness, ___ a crea-ture void ___ of form. _____ "Come

in," she said, "I'll give ya shel-ter from ___ the

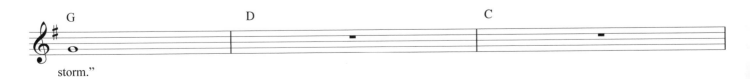

storm."

2. And

Additional Lyrics

2. And if I pass this way again, you can rest assured
   I'll always do my best for her; on that I give my word.
   In a world of steel-eyed death and men who are fighting to be warm,
   "Come in," she said, "I'll give ya shelter from the storm."

3. Not a word was spoke between us; there was little risk involved.
   Everything up to that point had been left unresolved.
   Try imagining a place where it's always safe and warm.
   "Come in," she said, "I'll give ya shelter from the storm."

4. I was burned out from exhaustion, buried in the hail,
   Poisoned in the bushes and blown out on the trail,
   Hunted like a crocodile, ravaged in the corn.
   "Come in," she said, "I'll give ya shelter from the storm."

5. Suddenly, I turned around and she was standin' there
   With silver bracelets on her wrists and flowers in her hair.
   She walked up to me so gracefully and took my crown of thorns.
   "Come in," she said, "I'll give ya shelter from the storm."

6. Now there's a wall between us; somethin' there's been lost.
   I took too much for granted; I got my signals crossed.
   Just to think that it all began on a non-eventful morn.
   "Come in," she said, "I'll give ya shelter from the storm."

7. Well, the deputy walks on hard nails and the preacher rides a mount,
   But nothing really matters much; it's doom alone that counts.
   And the one-eyed undertaker, he blows a futile horn.
   "Come in," she said, "I'll give ya shelter from the storm."

8. I've heard newborn babies wailin' like a mournin' dove
   And old men with broken teeth stranded without love.
   Do I understand your question, man? Is it hopeless and forlorn?
   "Come in," she said, "I'll give ya shelter from the storm."

9. In a little hilltop village, they gambled for my clothes.
   I bargained for salvation and she gave me a lethal dose.
   I offered up my innocence; I got repaid with scorn.
   "Come in," she said, "I'll give ya shelter from the storm."

10. Well, I'm livin' in a foreign country, but I'm bound to cross the line.
    Beauty walks a razor's edge; someday I'll make it mine.
    If I could only turn back the clock to when God and her were born.
    "Come in," she said, "I'll give ya shelter from the storm."

Singing the Blues

Words and Music by Melvin Endsley

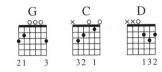

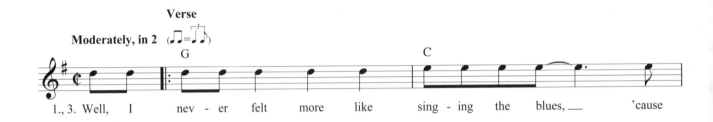

1., 3. Well, I nev - er felt more like sing - ing the blues, __ 'cause

I nev - er thought __ that I'd ev - er lose __ your love, dear.

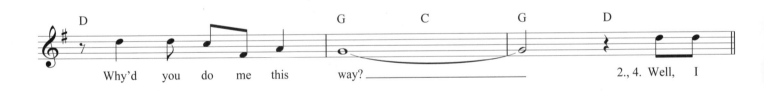

Why'd you do me this way? _____ 2., 4. Well, I

nev - er felt more like cry - ing all night, __ 'cause ev - 'ry - thing's wrong __ and

noth - ing ain't right __ with - out you. You got me sing - ing the

Bridge

blues. _____ The moon and stars no long - er shine, the

dream is gone I thought was mine. There's noth - ing left for

me to do but cry _____ o - ver you. ___ Well, I

Outro-Verse

nev - er felt more like run - ning a - way. ___ But why should I go, ___ 'cause

I could - n't stay ___ with - out you. You got me sing - ing the

|1. |2.

G   C   G   D   G

blues. _____ 3. Well, I   blues. _____

Thirty Days in the Hole

Words and Music by Steve Marriott

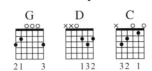

Verse
Moderately

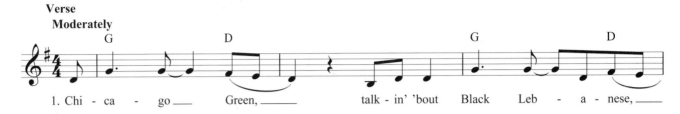

1. Chi - ca - go Green, talk - in' 'bout Black Leb - a - nese,

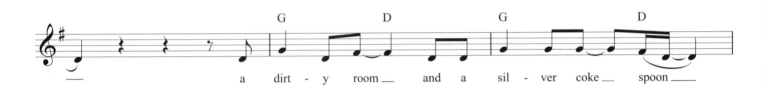

a dirt - y room and a sil - ver coke spoon

give me my re - lease. Black Nap - a - lese,

it's got you weak in your knees.

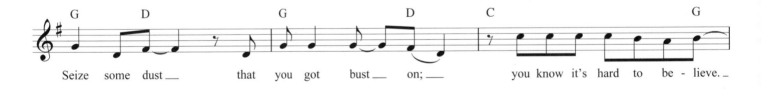

Seize some dust that you got bust on; you know it's hard to be - lieve.

% Chorus

Play 3 times

Thir - ty days in the hole, thir - ty days in the

Verse
To Coda

hole. 2. New - cas - tle Brown, I'm tell - ing you, can

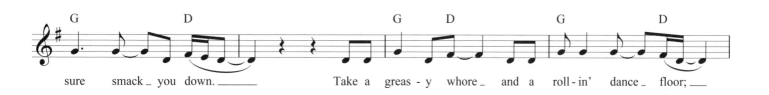

sure smack _ you down. _____ Take a greas-y whore _ and a roll-in' dance _ floor; ___

it's got your head spin-nin' 'round. _____ If you live on ___ the road, well, there's a

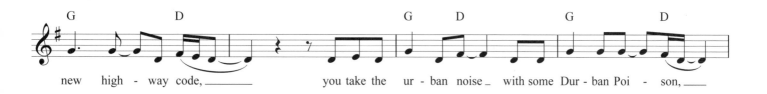

new high - way code, _____ you take the ur - ban noise _ with some Dur - ban Poi - son, ___

D.S. al Coda
(with repeats)

✛ Coda
Verse

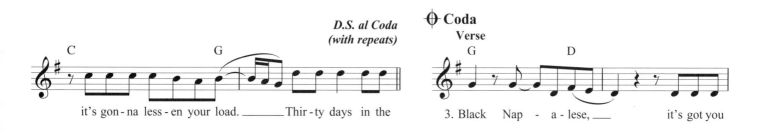

it's gon-na less-en your load. _____ Thir-ty days in the

3. Black Nap - a - lese, ___ it's got you

weak in ___ your knees. _____ Gon-na seize some dust _ that you got bust _ on, ___

you know it's so hard to please. New - cas - tle Brown _____ can

sure smack _ you down. _____ You take a greas-y whore _ and a roll-in' dance _ floor; ___

you know you're jail - house bound. _ Thir-ty days in the hole. _____

Three Little Birds

Words and Music by Bob Marley

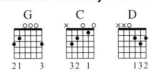

Don't wor - ry a - bout a thing, _____ 'cause

ev - 'ry lit - tle thing gon - na be al - right. _____ Sing - in', don't

wor - ry a - bout a thing, _____ 'cause

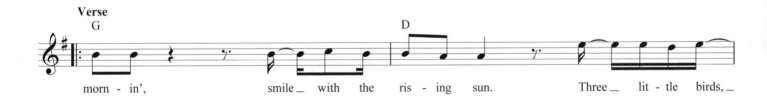

ev - 'ry lit - tle thing gon - na be al - right. _____ Rise up this

morn - in', smile _ with the ris - ing sun. Three _ lit - tle birds, _

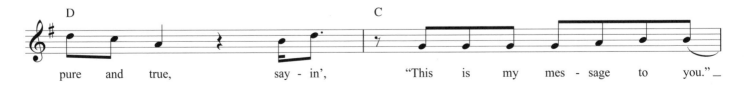

_ pitched by my door - step. Sing - in' sweet _ songs, of mel - o - dies

pure and true, say - in', "This is my mes - sage to you." _

Chorus

Sing - in', don't wor - ry a - bout a thing, ___

'cause ev - 'ry lit - tle thing is gon - na be al - right. ___

Sing - in', don't wor - ry, don't wor - ry 'bout a thing, ___

'cause ev - 'ry lit - tle thing gon - na be al - right. ___

1. Rise up this ___

2. Hmm, don't

Outro-Chorus

wor - ry a - bout a thing, ___ 'cause, uh,

ev - 'ry lit - tle thing is gon - na be al - right. ___ I won't wor - ry. Ba - by, don't

wor - ry a - bout a thing, ___ 'cause

Repeat and fade

ev - 'ry lit - tle thing is gon - na be al - right. ___ Say, ___ don't

Too Much

Words and Music by Lee Rosenberg and Bernard Weinman

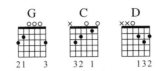

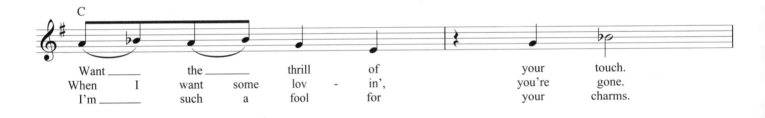

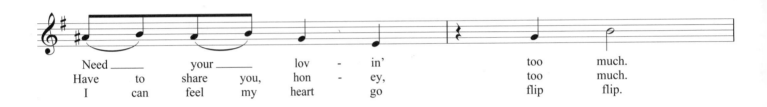

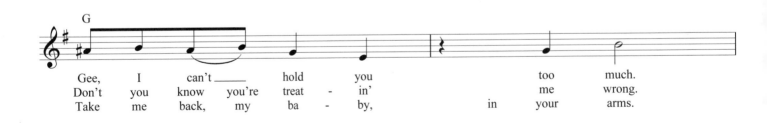

love you too much.
love you too
love you too

Chorus

Need _____ your _____ lov - in' _____ all the time. _____

Need _____ your _____ hug - gin'; _____ please be mine. _____

Need _____ you _____ near me; _____ stay real close. _____

Please, _____ please, _____ hear me; _____ you're the most. _____

Now you got me start - ed; don't you leave me bro - ken - heart - ed 'cause I

To Coda 🔶   *D.C. al Coda*
                    (take 2nd ending)   🔶 **Coda**

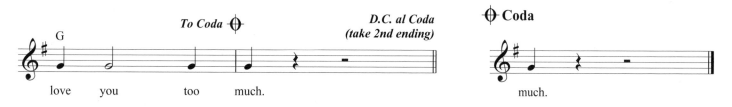

love you too much.   much.

Walk of Life

Words and Music by Mark Knopfler

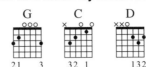

Verse
Moderately, in 2

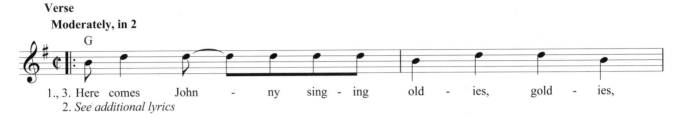

1., 3. Here comes John - ny sing - ing old - ies, gold - ies,
2. *See additional lyrics*

be - bop - a - lu - la, ba - by, what I say.___ Here comes John - ny sing - ing,

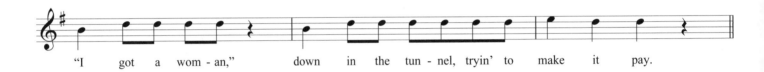

"I got a wom - an," down in the tun - nel, tryin' to make it pay.

Chorus

1. He got the ac - tion, he got the mo - tion. Oh yeah, ___ the
2., 3. *See additional lyrics*

boy can play. Ded - i - ca - tion, ___ de - vo - tion,

turn - ing all the night - time in - to the day. ___ He do the song a - bout the sweet lov - in'

wom - an, he do the song a - bout the knife. Then he do the walk,

he   do   the   walk   of   life.   Yeah, —   he   do   the   walk   of   life. _____

(Instrumental)

Outro

Repeat and fade

Additional Lyrics

2. Here comes Johnny, gonna tell you the story;
   Hand me down my walkin' shoes.
   Here comes Johnny with the power and the glory,
   Back-beat the talkin' blues.

Chorus 2: He got the action, he got the motion.
   Oh yeah, the boy can play.
   Dedication, devotion,
   Turning all the nighttime into the day.
   He do the song about the sweet lovin' woman,
   He do the song about the knife.
   Then he do the walk, he do the walk of life.
   Yeah, he do the walk of life.

Chorus 3: He got the action, he got the motion,
   Yeah, the boy can play;
   Dedication, devotion,
   Turning all the nighttime into the day.
   And after all the violence and double talk,
   There's just a song in all the trouble and the strife.
   You do the walk, you do the walk of life.
   Mmm you do the walk of life.

You'll Accomp'ny Me

Words and Music by Bob Seger

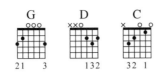

Verse
Moderately

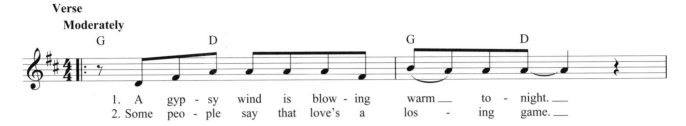

1. A gyp - sy wind is blow - ing warm __ to - night. __
2. Some peo - ple say that love's a los - ing game. __

The sky is star - lit and the time is right. __
You start with fi - re, but you lose the flame. __

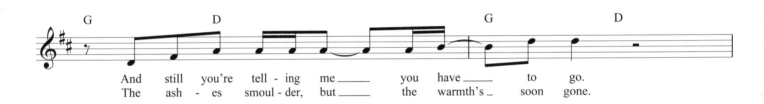

And still you're tell - ing me __ you have __ to go.
The ash - es smoul - der, but __ the warmth's _ soon gone.

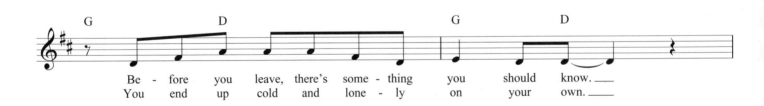

Be - fore you leave, there's some - thing you should know. __
You end up cold and lone - ly on your own. __

I've seen you smil - ing in the sum - mer sun.
I'll take my chanc - es, babe. I'll risk it all.

I've seen your long hair fly - ing when you run. __
I'll win your love or I'll take the fall. __

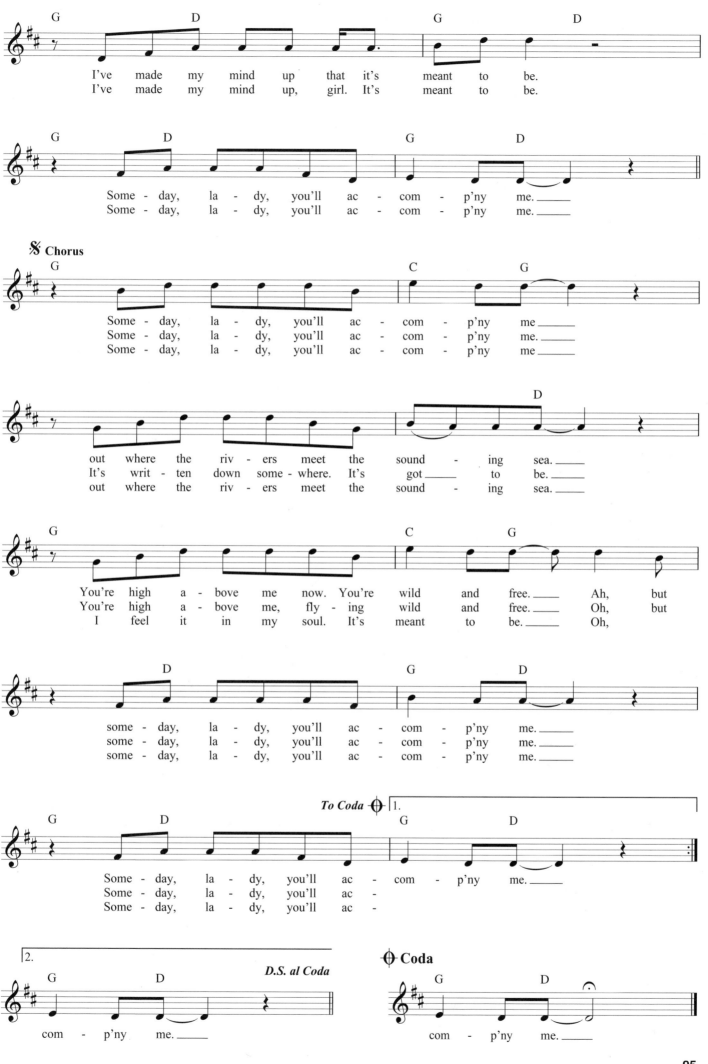

HAL LEONARD GUITAR CHEAT SHEETS

The Hal Leonard Cheat Sheets series includes lyrics, chord frames, and "rhythm tab" (cut-to-the-chase notation) to make playing easier than ever! No music reading is required, and all the songs are presented on two-page spreads to avoid page turns.

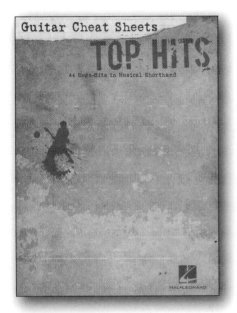

TOP HITS

44 pop favorites, including: Are You Gonna Be My Girl • Baby • Bad Day • Bubbly • Clocks • Crazy • Fireflies • Gives You Hell • Hey, Soul Sister • How to Save a Life • I Gotta Feeling Just the Way You Are • Lucky • Mercy • Mr. Brightside • Need You Now • Take Me Out • Toes • Use Somebody • Viva La Vida • You Belong with Me • and more.
00701646 ....$14.99

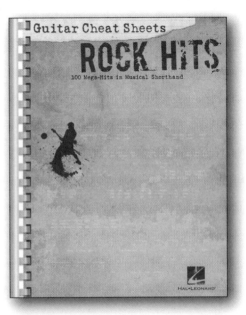

ROCK HITS

44 songs, including: Are You Gonna Go My Way • Black Hole Sun • Counting Blue Cars • Float On • Friday I'm in Love • Gives You Hell • Grenade • Jeremy • Kryptonite • Push • Scar Tissue • Semi-Charmed Life • Smells like Teen Spirit • Smooth • Thnks Fr Th Mmrs • Two Princes • Use Somebody • Viva La Vida • Where Is the Love • You Oughta Know • and more.
00702392 ....$24.99

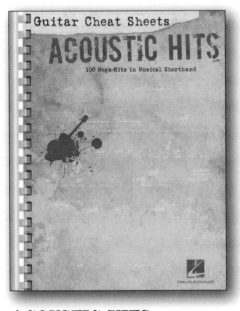

ACOUSTIC HITS

100 unplugged megahits in musical shorthand: All Apologies • Crazy Little Thing Called Love • Creep • Daughter • Every Rose Has Its Thorn • Hallelujah • I'm Yours • The Lazy Song • Little Lion Man • Love Story • More Than Words • Patience • Strong Enough • 21 Guns • Wanted Dead or Alive • Wonderwall • and more.
00702391 ....$24.99

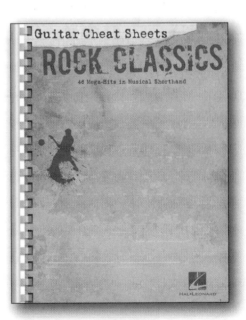

ROCK CLASSICS

Nearly 50 classics, including: All Right Now • Barracuda • Born to Be Wild • Carry on Wayward Son • Cat Scratch Fever • Free Ride • Layla • Message in a Bottle • Paranoid • Proud Mary • Rhiannon • Rock and Roll All Nite • Slow Ride • Smoke on the Water • Sweet Home Alabama • Welcome to the Jungle • You Shook Me All Night Long • and more.
00702393 ....$24.99

HAL•LEONARD® CORPORATION
7777 W. BLUEMOUND RD. P.O. BOX 13819 MILWAUKEE, WI 53213

Visit Hal Leonard online at **www.halleonard.com**   *Prices, contents, and availability subject to change without notice.*   0712